MILK

Dorothy Turner

Illustrations by John Yates

Carolrhoda Books, Inc./Minneapolis

All words that appear in **bold** are
explained in the glossary on page 30.

First published in the U.S. in 1989 by
Carolrhoda Books, Inc.

LIBRARY OF CONGRESS
Library of Congress Cataloging-in-Publication Data

Turner, Dorothy.
  Milk / Dorothy Turner ; illustrations by John Yates.
    p. cm.
  Bibliography: p.
  Includes index.
  Summary: Discusses the processing, distribution, and nutritional
value of milk and milk products, such as cheese, butter, and
yogurt. Includes ice cream and yogurt recipes.
  ISBN 0-87614-361-3 (lib. bdg.)
  1. Milk—Juvenile literature. 2. Dairy products—Juvenile
literature. [1. Milk. 2. Dairy products.] I. Yates, John, ill.
II. Title.
SF239.5.T87   1989
637′.1—dc19   88-25144
                                                          CIP
                                                           AC

Printed in Italy by G. Canale C.S.p.A., Turin
Bound in the United States of America

1 2 3 4 5 6 7 8 9 10 99 98 97 96 95 94 93 92 91 90 89

Contents

sheep

The milk we drink

People have used milk in one form or another since the beginning of history. Foods made from milk, such as cheese, butter, and soured milk, are believed to have been eaten by the peoples who roamed the grasslands of Asia with their cattle and sheep thousands of years ago.

Although the most common kind of milk comes from cows, cow's milk is not the only kind of milk

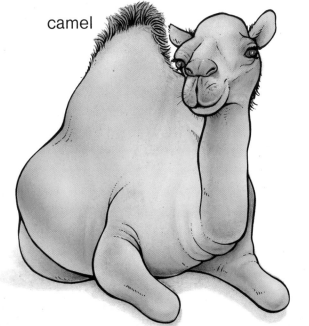
camel

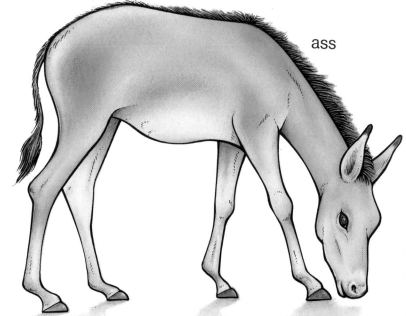
ass

people use. It is hard to raise cows in mountainous and desert areas where there is no grass for them to eat. In these places, people often use the milk of other animals.

Almost half of the milk drunk in India comes from the water buffalo. Buffalo milk is also drunk in China, Egypt, and the Philippines. Reindeer milk is drunk in northern Europe. In other countries, people drink milk from goats, sheep, asses, camels, llamas, yaks, and even horses.

llama

reindeer

5

An important food

Milk builds strong and healthy bodies.

Every one of us begins our life drinking milk. It might be human milk from our mother, milk from a cow or other animal, or baby food made from dried cow's milk. Both humans and cows are **mammals**—milk-producing animals. All mammals, from creatures as large as whales to those as small as mice, produce milk in **mammary glands.** Babies suck at these glands to get milk. Each mammal produces milk that contains just the right ingredients for its babies.

Milk is one of the most important foods in the world. Although milk is mostly made up of water, it also contains other substances we need to stay healthy. It has fats and carbohydrates, which give us energy. It has protein, which helps us grow and

avoid illness. Milk is also a rich source of vitamins and minerals. These provide us with energy and help to build strong muscles, bones, and teeth.

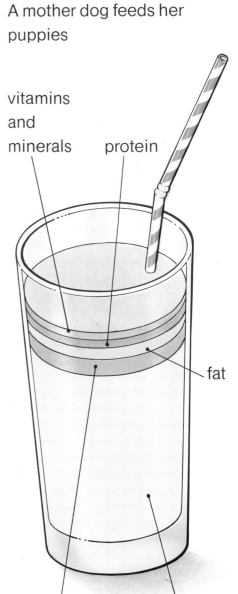

A mother dog feeds her puppies

vitamins and minerals

protein

fat

carbohydrates   water

Dairy farming

Not long ago, most cows were raised on small farms. Sometimes a family would have just one cow to provide them with milk. While some farmers still raise only a few cows at a time, today, most dairy farming is big business. Modern dairy farms have hundreds of cows that produce gallons and gallons of milk each day.

A farmer exercises his dairy cows on his farm in Normandy, France.

guernsey

jersey

holstein

Dairy cattle are raised throughout the world, wherever there is a supply of grass. Certain breeds of cattle have been developed that produce large amounts of milk. These include guernsey, jersey, holstein, and Ayrshire.

Before a cow can produce milk, it must first give birth to a calf. After the calf is born, the cow produces milk for about 10 months. Farmers usually arrange for each cow to have one calf every year so that there is a constant supply of milk.

How cows produce milk

A dairy cow chewing grass. Notice how her udder is full of milk.

If you have ever watched a cow, you will have seen that it spends a great deal of time chewing. What it is doing is, in fact, turning the grass or special feed it eats into milk.

In some countries, such as New Zealand, cows have a fresh supply of grass all year round. In other countries, they eat grass in the summer and special feed in the winter. Some cows will eat as much as 210 pounds of food in one day.

Unlike a human being, a cow has four compartments in its stomach. When a cow eats, it swallows its food quickly, without chewing it well. The food is stored in the first two stomach compartments.

Later, when the cow has finished eating, it uses its stomach muscles to bring the unchewed food back to its mouth, a little bit at a time. Then the cow chews the food completely. This is called chewing

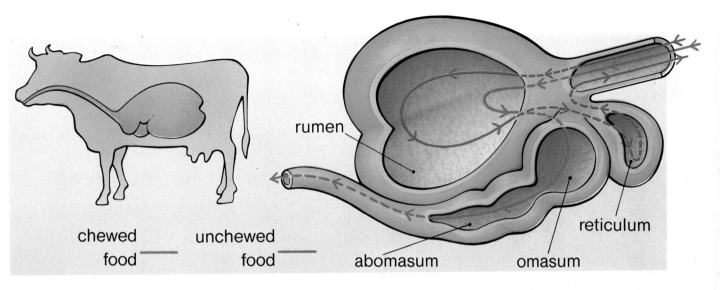

rumen

chewed food ___ unchewed food ___

abomasum

omasum

reticulum

the **cud.** The cow swallows the food again, and it goes to the animal's third and fourth stomach compartments. There, water is removed and special juices help to digest, or break down, the food.

Some of the digested food is turned into milk in the **udder.** The udder is a milk bag that hangs from the cow's body just in front of its hind legs. It has four large nipples called **teats.** When the udder is full, the cow is ready to be milked.

This diagram shows the four compartments of a cow's stomach. The un-chewed grass is stored in the *rumen* and *reticulum.* Any water is removed in the *omasum.* The grass is broken down by digestive juices in the *abomasum.*

Milking

Above: A dairy farm in Australia

Right: Milking a goat by hand in Mongolia

Cows like a settled routine. Twice a day, early in the morning and in the evening, they are brought in from the fields to be milked. If this routine is broken, the cows produce less milk. A healthy cow gives as much as 1,200 gallons of milk in one year.

At one time, all cows were milked by hand. In many parts of the world, people still milk cows the old-fashioned way. The person doing the milking

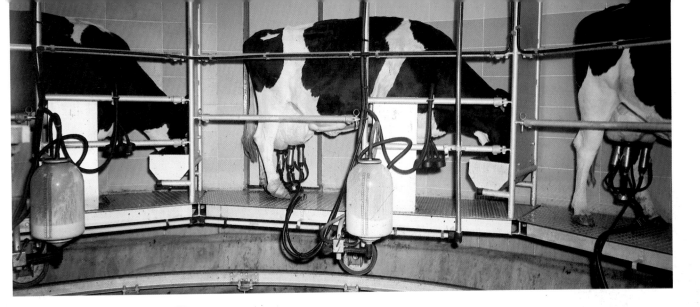

sits beside the cow and squeezes the milk out of the animal's teats into a bucket. But milking by hand is quite slow, so large dairy farms use milking machines instead. At milking time, the cows are taken to a special farm building. There they are lined up, and electric milking machines are attached to their udders. The machines painlessly pump the milk out of the teats. After the milk is measured, it is refrigerated until it can be collected by tanker trucks.

Milking machines are used on large dairy farms. A milking machine is attached to each cow's udder, and then the milk is pumped out of the teats.

13

At the dairy

The trucks take the milk from the farm to a dairy. There it is weighed and checked for freshness. The amount of fat the milk contains is also checked.

Milk is full of bits of fat called **butterfat.** The fat floats on top because it is lighter than the rest of the milk. The top layer of milk is called cream.

The more butterfat that milk has, the more the farmer is paid for the milk.

At the dairy, different amounts of butterfat are

A dairy in Kenya

removed to make different kinds of milk. In **whole milk,** all the butterfat is left in. Milk that has most of the butterfat removed is called **low-fat milk. Skim milk** has all but a tiny amount of butterfat taken out.

Today, yogurt is very popular and many different flavors are available. People often eat low-fat yogurt as a diet food. Frozen yogurt, which is similar to ice cream, is eaten as a dessert.

Processing milk

Louis Pasteur, the famous French scientist, working in his laboratory

Milk that has come right from the cow is not always safe to drink. This caused many problems for people in the past. There was something in

milk that made it spoil very quickly. Even worse, milk also contained something that caused diseases, such as tuberculosis and typhoid. Many people died from these diseases, but no one knew what caused them or how they could be prevented.

In the 19th century, a French scientist named Louis Pasteur discovered that both the diseases and the spoiled milk were caused by bacteria, or germs, in the milk. He found that if milk is heated, but not boiled, the disease-producing bacteria in it are destroyed. Heating the milk also slows the growth of the bacteria that make milk spoil.

This process is called **pasteurization**, and it is still used today. Milk is heated to 161°F (72°C) for 15 seconds. Then it is quickly cooled and kept refrigerated until it is needed. Louis Pasteur's discovery saved many lives and led to the development of the modern dairy industry.

Some milk is given another kind of treatment

Testing milk to make sure all the bacteria has been destroyed

This diagram shows a modern pasteurizing machine, which removes the bacteria from milk.

that makes it safe to drink. The **ultrahigh-temperature,** or **UHT, process** is like pasteurization but uses much higher heat. The milk is heated to about 300°F (149°C) for six to nine seconds. It is cooled rapidly and put in airtight containers. Milk that has been processed this way will stay fresh for up to a few months. UHT milk is also called **sterilized milk.**

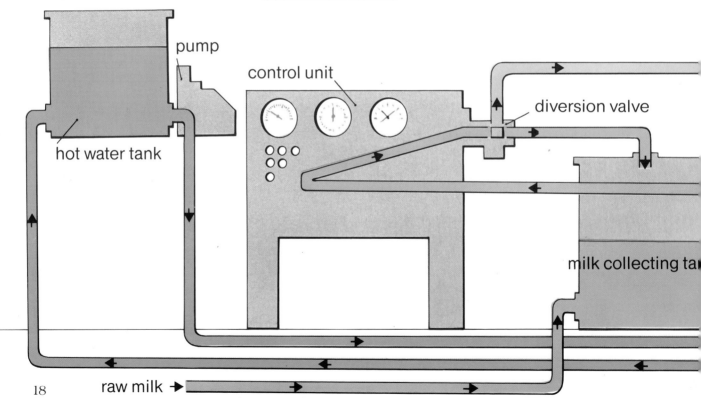

pump

control unit

diversion valve

hot water tank

milk collecting ta

raw milk →

In the final step at a dairy, milk is put into cartons or plastic containers and shipped to grocery stores. Dairies are always extremely clean. The floors, walls, tanks, and pipes are kept spotless.

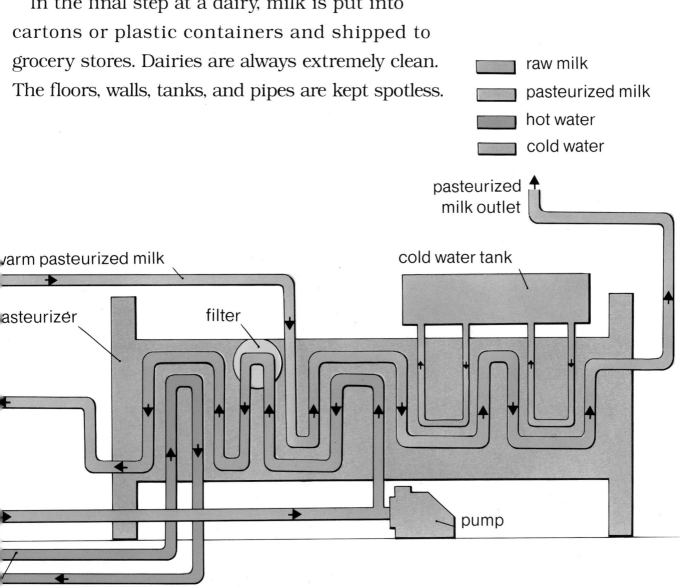

raw milk

pasteurized milk

hot water

cold water

pasteurized milk outlet

warm pasteurized milk

cold water tank

pasteurizer

filter

pump

hot water tubes

Cheese

Milk is the basis of many other foods, including cheese. Most cheese is made by adding **rennet** to fresh milk. Rennet is a liquid that comes from a calf's stomach. It causes milk to separate into white lumps and a watery liquid. The lumps are

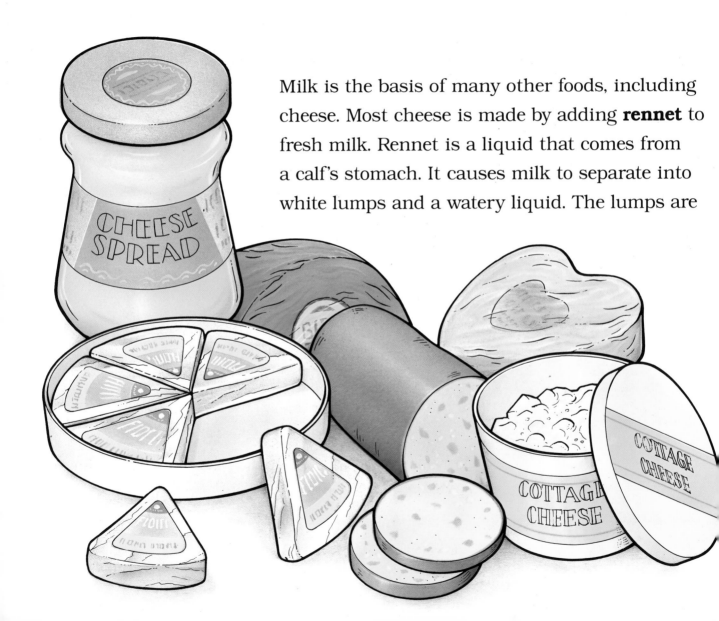

called **curd.** The liquid is called **whey.** When the curd is left to harden, it becomes cheese.

There are hundreds of varieties of cheese, made by adding different flavors and colors. Blue cheese is made by adding mold to cheese. The mold forms blue lines in the cheese and gives it a strong flavor. Blue cheese is a hard cheese. There are also many kinds of soft cheese, such as cottage cheese and cream cheese.

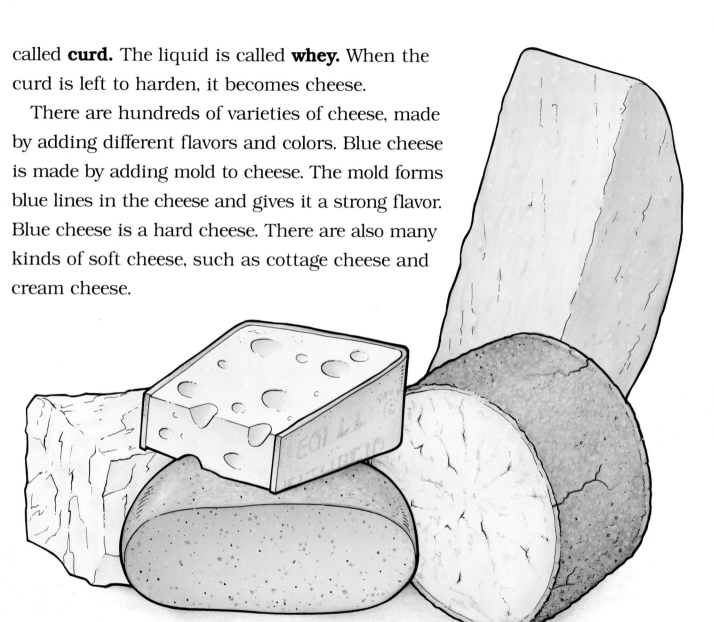

Butter and yogurt

Above: Cooking
with yogurt

Below: People of all ages
enjoy yogurt.

Butter was not always used just for cooking or eating. The ancient Greeks and Romans believed it could heal wounds. They also put it in their hair as a sort of gel. In Scotland, butter was used as oil for lamps as recently as the 19th century.

Butter is made from cream. Huge machines are used to churn, or stir, the cream until the butterfat in the cream sticks together to form butter. The liquid that is left behind is poured off. The butter is washed, cut into bars, and packaged for sale in grocery stores.

Yogurt is another food we get from milk. It is made by adding two special kinds of bacteria to milk. As the bacteria grow, they cause a change to take place. They turn the milk into a soft, slightly sour food we call yogurt.

Making butter for sale at a market in Addis Ababa, Ethiopia

Other milk products

Most children like milk, especially if it has been flavored with chocolate.

Milk comes in many forms besides whole, low-fat, or skim. **Evaporated milk** is made by heating milk until about half the water in it is gone. Then the milk is sealed in germ-free cans. Canned milk does not have to be kept cold, and it will not spoil until after the can is opened.

Condensed milk has much of its water removed, but the milk also has a large amount of sugar added to it. The sugar gives the milk a sweet taste and also stops bacteria from growing and spoiling the milk. Condensed milk is often used in baking.

Skim milk is sometimes made into **powdered milk.** The milk is heated until all the water is gone, leaving only powder. The powder dissolves back into liquid milk when water is added to it.

Skim milk can also be turned into **buttermilk.**
The milk is treated with certain bacteria that
change it into a rather thick, smooth liquid with
a sour taste.

Ice cream is a popular treat
made from milk.

Make sure there is an adult nearby when you are cooking.

Make your own yogurt

You will need:

a wide-necked vacuum bottle
about 3 cups sterilized milk
2 tablespoons plain yogurt

2. Put yogurt into the vacuum bottle. Slowly add milk while gently stirring the mixture.

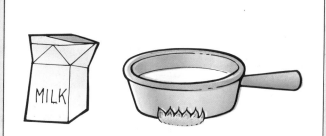

1. Measure enough milk to fill ¾ of the vacuum bottle. Pour milk into a small pan and heat very gently until it is lukewarm. Ask an adult to test how warm the milk is. Do not let the milk get too hot.

3. Screw the lid tightly back on the vacuum bottle. Let it stand for at least 8 hours. Then pour the yogurt into a bowl and store in the refrigerator. Eat it plain or with jam, fruit, or granola stirred in.

An East Indian yogurt recipe: raita

You will need:
¾ cup plain yogurt
1/2 small cucumber
a handful of mint leaves

2. Beat the yogurt until it is smooth, add the chopped ingredients, and stir.

1. Slice the cucumber thinly, and finely chop the mint. Remember to ask an adult to help you when using a knife.

3. Chill the raita at least an hour before serving.

Make your own ice cream

You will need:
4 egg whites
1/2 cup sugar
4 egg yolks
3¼ cups whipping cream
1 teaspoon vanilla extract

2. Beat the cream until it is stiff.

1. Beat the egg whites until they are stiff. Add the sugar little by little, beating all the time.

3. Stir the egg yolks together until they are runny.

28

- 1 teaspoon peppermint flavoring and a few drops green food coloring
- 1/2 cup each of chopped nuts and raisins that have been soaked in orange juice
- 1 cup chocolate chips
- a melted chocolate bar mixed with 1 tablespoon of milk. Don't add this mixture until ice cream is nearly frozen.

4. Stir the egg whites, cream, and egg yolks together. Add the vanilla extract and stir. You can also try one of the following flavorings instead of vanilla:

5. Pour the ice cream into a plastic container and freeze.

Glossary

butterfat: bits of fat in milk

buttermilk: a thick, smooth, sour-tasting milk made by adding certain bacteria to skim milk

condensed milk: a sweet milk made by removing some of the water from milk and adding sugar

cud: food brought up from a cow's stomach that the cow chews again

curd: the lumps that form when rennet is added to milk

evaporated milk: milk with half of the water removed

low-fat milk: milk with most of the butterfat removed

mammals: animals that produce milk for their young

mammary glands: organs that produce milk

pasteurization: a process that uses heat to kill the bacteria in milk

powdered milk: milk that has had all of the water removed, leaving only a powder

rennet: a liquid that comes from a calf's stomach that is used in making cheese

skim milk: milk with all but a tiny bit of butterfat removed

sterilized milk: milk in which the bacteria have been destroyed by the ultrahigh-temperature (UHT) process

teats: nipples. A cow has four large teats on its udder.

udder: a baglike part of the cow's body that stores the milk the animal produces

ultrahigh-temperature (UHT) process: a process that uses very high heat to kill the bacteria in milk

whey: the watery liquid formed when rennet is added to milk

whole milk: milk with none of the butterfat removed

Index

Photo Acknowledgments

The photographs in this book were provided by: pp. 6, 10, ZEFA; pp. 8, 12, (right),17, 22 (bottom), 25, Hutchison Library; pp. 12 (top), 23, Christine Osborne; pp. 13, 15, 22 (top), Topham Picture Library; p. 16, Mary Evans Picture Library; p. 24, Sally and Richard Greenhill. Cover photograph by Peter Stiles.